W9-BIC-570

® Landoll, Inc.
Ashland, Ohio 44805
LOONEY TUNES, characters, names, and all related
indicia are trademarks of Warner Bros., Inc. © 1997.
No part of this book may be reproduced or copied.
All Rights Reserved. Made in the U.S.A. LAN232

STORYBOOK

Elmer Fudd's CELLAR

by Julie McNally

Illustrated by Sol Studios, Argentina and
Landoll, Inc.

Elmer Fudd's new house was a marvel to behold, and now Elmer was ready to move in.

"Time for me to start putting away my badminton books, my sowar-heated hat, and my ewectwic tambourine cowwection."

Elmer picked up a box marked CELLAR.

"The cewwar?!" Elmer exclaimed. "You know,
I forgot to build a cewwar."

Elmer got a shovel and a jackhammer and marked a big **X** on the floor of his kitchen. "This would be a perfect place for a cewwar." He started up the jackhammer. **RRAAAAA–BBBBUDDABUDDA BUDDA!**

The jackhammer shook and roared,
making the ground quake. Elmer didn't know that he had
built his new house directly over someone else's home:
Bugs Bunny's rabbit hole.

"Hey! What's the big idea?!" Bugs yelled over the noisy jackhammer. His little rabbit hole of a house was shaking like the engine in an old car. Then a chunk of Bugs's ceiling fell in.

Bugs walked over to inspect his fallen ceiling. "Hmmm . . . termites," he concluded.

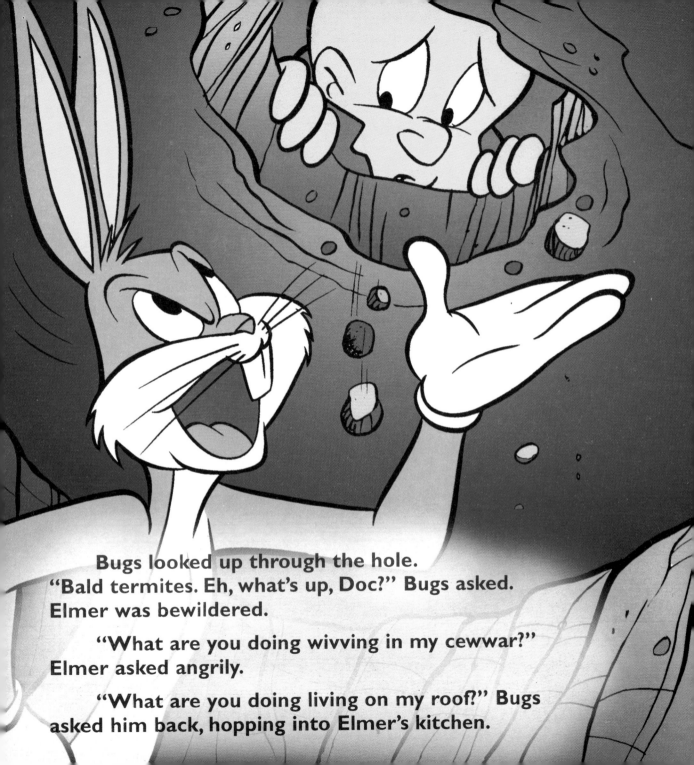

Bugs looked up through the hole.
"Bald termites. Eh, what's up, Doc?" Bugs asked.
Elmer was bewildered.

"What are you doing wivving in my cewwar?"
Elmer asked angrily.

"What are you doing living on my roof?" Bugs
asked him back, hopping into Elmer's kitchen.

"Why, you scwewy rabbit! This is my house, and you're twespassing!"

"I'd say it's you who's doing the trespassing, pal," said Bugs, helping himself to a carrot from Elmer's refrigerator.

"Listen, Doc—you seem like a nice fella, so I'm gonna make you a deal," said Bugs, leaning in very close to Elmer's face.

"Yes? What is it?" asked Elmer, who was interested.

"GET OUT!" Bugs screamed at the top of his lungs. As Elmer stood rubbing his ear, Bugs hopped back down into his rabbit hole.

"Why you . . ." hollered Elmer as he grabbed his jackhammer and started again.
BRAAAAAAAAAABUDDABUDDABUDDA!

Suddenly, Elmer felt a tap on his shoulder. "Jackhammer inspector," said the man, whose long ears stuck out of the back of his work helmet. "I need to see your license, pal."

"Wicense? For a jackhammer? But I don't have one," Elmer said. He was sweating now.

"Operatin' a jackhammer without a license, eh?" the inspector said. "That's a $1000 fine."

"A thousand dowwars?!"

"And your jackhammering privileges
are revoked," he said as he took Elmer's
jackhammer and walked away.

"Hey! You're no jackhammer inspector!" yelled Elmer. He grabbed his shovel. Bugs ran up next to him and began digging from the pile of dirt Elmer was making, throwing it back into the hole.

"I'll fix that wabbit," Elmer said. CRASH!
WHOOSH! He took a steamshovel and caved
in Bugs's ceiling. Of course, this meant **WAR**.

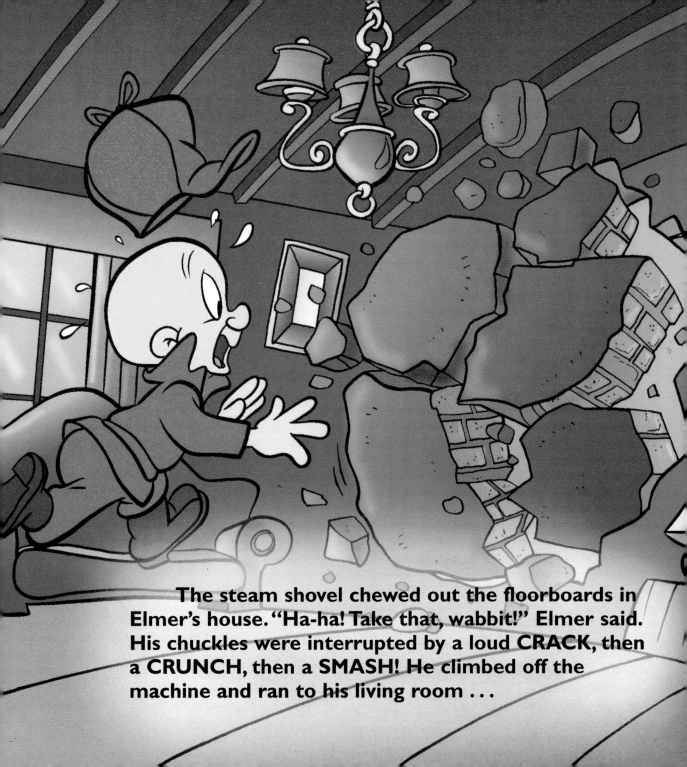

The steam shovel chewed out the floorboards in Elmer's house. "Ha-ha! Take that, wabbit!" Elmer said. His chuckles were interrupted by a loud **CRACK**, then a **CRUNCH**, then a **SMASH**! He climbed off the machine and ran to his living room . . .

"Need some help?" Bugs asked.

Elmer tried to chase Bugs, but the bunny was too fast. Elmer climbed back on the steamshovel and tried to drive the machine out of his living room, but went backwards through his bedroom. "My new house!" he cried.

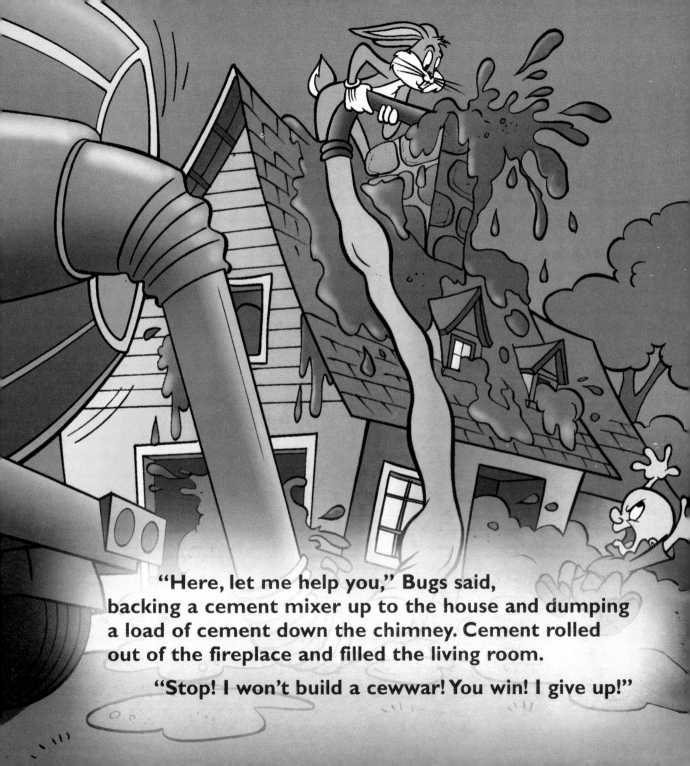

"Here, let me help you," Bugs said, backing a cement mixer up to the house and dumping a load of cement down the chimney. Cement rolled out of the fireplace and filled the living room.

"Stop! I won't build a cewwar! You win! I give up!"

"Good," Bugs said. "I almost rented a subway-tunnel digger. I need a new bathroom in my place."

"I think I'll build an attic instead," Elmer said.

"Not if I've got anything to say about it," a voice said from the ceiling.

Elmer and Bugs looked up to see Daffy Duck resting on a hammock.

"There's six more weeks of winter where I'm from, and I'm not going back till spring!" declared the duck. Elmer ran screaming and crying down the street. "Well, there goes the neighborhood," Daffy said.